simple
salads

THE AUSTRALIAN
Women's Weekly

CONTENTS

Australian cup and spoon measurements are metric. A conversion chart appears on page 77.

Salads make terrific starters and sides, but they also make great main courses too, especially if they're to be served to a large number of people; most of the preparation can be done beforehand, then it's simply a matter of tossing the ingredients together at the last minute.

Pamela Clark

Food Director

SENSATIONAL SALADS

Salads are wonderfully versatile – they can be served as a starter, side dish or an impressive main meal. And with the increasing availability of once exotic salad vegetables in our supermarkets, our salads have become much more interesting.

Storing leaves
Store lettuce and salad leaves in the crisper of your refrigerator. Store fresh herbs in the fridge standing upright in a glass or jug half-filled with water and covered with a plastic bag. Throw them out once they wilt.

Storing tomatoes and avocados
Tomatoes and avocados won't ripen after chilling, so always store them at room temperature. Once ripe you can store avocados in the fridge for a day or two, but tomatoes always taste better if kept at room temperature.

Which dressing?

A complex salad is best served with a simple vinaigrette; a sharp vinegary dressing is good on tomato salads, while a creamy dressing works best with soft or crisp salad leaves.

How much dressing?

The biggest mistake people make with salads is that they use too much dressing. Just before serving, pour on about half as much dressing as you think you'll need and toss the salad. You can always add a little more later, but too much dressing will produce a soggy salad.

Salad seed mixtures

These are wonderful sprinkled over salads – and with steamed or baked vegetables. You can buy ready-made mixtures at some greengrocers and supermarkets, but if you want to make your own, follow this delicious recipe:

Dry-fry 100g each of sesame seeds, sunflower seeds and pepitas (pumpkin seeds) along with 40g pine nuts. Stir constantly, until the sesame seeds start to pop and the remaining ingredients toast slightly. Don't take your eyes off them because they can burn in an instant. Put them into a bowl and pour 1 tablespoon of soy sauce over them while they're still hot, tossing to coat thoroughly. Store in an airtight container in the fridge.

LEMON GARLIC CHICKEN ON CIABATTA

prep & cook time 15 minutes serves 4
nutritional count per serving 20.1g total fat
(3.8g saturated fat); 1438kJ (344 cal);
15.8g carbohydrate; 24.5g protein; 1.3g fibre

1 litre (4 cups) water
400g chicken breast fillets
4 thick slices ciabatta bread (140g)
1 tablespoon olive oil
1 clove garlic, crushed
lemon, chilli and parsley dressing
2 tablespoons olive oil
2 teaspoons finely grated lemon rind
1 fresh long red chilli, chopped finely
2 tablespoons finely chopped fresh
    flat-leaf parsley

1 Bring the water to the boil in large frying pan;
add chicken. Reduce heat; simmer, covered,
about 10 minutes or until chicken is cooked.
Cool chicken in poaching liquid 10 minutes;
drain, shred chicken finely.
2 Meanwhile, preheat grill to hot.
3 Brush bread both sides with combined oil
and garlic; toast, both sides, under grill.
4 Make lemon, chilli and parsley dressing.
5 Combine chicken and dressing in large bowl;
divide among toasts.
lemon, chilli and parsley dressing Combine
ingredients in screw-top jar; shake well.

SIDES &
STARTERS

ZUCCHINI AND RICOTTA PASTA SALAD

prep & cook time **25 minutes** serves **10**
nutritional count per serving **12.6g total fat**
(4g saturated fat); 1279kJ (306 cal);
35.g carbohydrate; 10.6g protein; 2.8g fibre

500g penne pasta
4 large zucchini (600g), sliced thinly
    lengthways
⅓ cup (80ml) olive oil
1 tablespoon finely grated lemon rind
⅓ cup (80ml) lemon juice
2 cloves garlic, crushed
400g ricotta cheese, crumbled
½ cup loosely packed fresh basil leaves,
    shredded finely

1 Cook pasta in large saucepan of boiling water
until tender; drain.
2 Meanwhile, combine zucchini and half the
oil in medium bowl. Cook zucchini, in batches,
on heated oiled grill plate (or grill or barbecue)
until tender.
3 Combine zucchini, rind, juice, garlic and
remaining oil in large bowl. Gently mix in pasta,
cheese and basil.

curried egg salad

CURRIED EGG SALAD

prep time **20 minutes** serves **4**
nutritional count per serving **15.2g total fat**
(3g saturated fat); 832kJ (199 cal);
6.1g carbohydrate; 9.3g protein; 1.2g fibre

1 stalk celery (150g), trimmed, cut into
    matchsticks
¼ small red onion (25g), sliced thinly
½ cup coarsely chopped fresh flat-leaf
    parsley
4 hard-boiled eggs, grated finely
4 small butter lettuce leaves, sliced thinly
curry mayonnaise
⅓ cup (100g) mayonnaise
1 tablespoon lemon juice
½ teaspoon curry powder

1 Make curry mayonnaise.
2 Combine celery, onion and parsley in
medium bowl. Top lettuce with egg then
celery mixture; drizzle with mayonnaise.
curry mayonnaise Combine ingredients in
small bowl.

zucchini and ricotta pasta salad

lemon & lime rice salad

LEMON & LIME RICE SALAD

prep & cook time **25 minutes** serves **8**
nutritional count per serving **17.7g total fat**
(2.1g saturated fat); 1505kJ (360 cal);
41.6g carbohydrate; 8.1g protein; 2.4g fibre

2 cups (400g) basmati rice
½ cup (80g) almond kernels,
    chopped coarsely
¼ cup (50g) pepitas
¼ cup (35g) sunflower seed kernels
½ cup finely sliced fresh coriander
½ cup finely sliced fresh flat-leaf parsley
lemon and lime dressing
¼ cup (60ml) olive oil
¼ cup (60ml) lemon juice
1 teaspoon finely grated lime rind
2 tablespoons lime juice
¼ teaspoon cracked black pepper

1 Cook rice in large saucepan of boiling water,
uncovered, until tender; drain. Rinse under cold
water; drain. Place in large bowl.
2 Meanwhile, make lemon & lime dressing.
3 Add dressing and remaining ingredients to
rice; mix gently.
lemon & lime dressing Combine ingredients
in screw-top jar; shake well.

wild rice salad with spinach & figs

WILD RICE SALAD WITH SPINACH & FIGS

prep & cook time **15 minutes** serves **8**
nutritional count per serving **13g total fat**
(1.2g saturated fat); 1359kJ (325 cal);
44.8g carbohydrate; 5.1g protein; 3.6g fibre

2 cups (400g) wild rice blend
¾ cup (90g) coarsely chopped pecans,
    roasted
½ cup (100g) thinly sliced dried figs
100g baby spinach leaves, chopped coarsely
2 green onions, sliced thinly
orange balsamic dressing
2 teaspoons finely grated orange rind
½ cup (125ml) orange juice
2 tablespoons olive oil
1 tablespoon white balsamic vinegar

1 Cook rice in large saucepan of boiling water,
uncovered, until tender; drain. Rinse under cold
water; drain. Place in large bowl.
2 Meanwhile, make orange balsamic dressing.
3 Add dressing and remaining ingredients to
rice; mix gently.
orange balsamic dressing Combine
ingredients in screw-top jar; shake well.

cabbage, orange & radish salad

WARM RED CABBAGE & BACON SALAD

prep & cook time **25 minutes** serves **4**
nutritional count per serving **9.2g total fat**
(2.2g saturated fat); 656kJ (157 cal);
7g carbohydrate; 9.1g protein; 5g fibre

2 rindless bacon rashers (130g),
   chopped coarsely
1 tablespoon olive oil
6 cups (480g) coarsely shredded
   red cabbage
2 tablespoons red wine vinegar
1 tablespoon brown sugar
½ cup coarsely chopped fresh
   flat-leaf parsley

1 Cook bacon in heated large frying pan until
crisp. Drain on absorbent paper.
2 Heat oil in same pan; cook cabbage, stirring,
about 5 minutes or until softened. Add vinegar
and sugar; cook, stirring, about 10 minutes or
until liquid evaporates.
3 Return bacon to pan; stir until heated through.
Remove from heat; stir in parsley.

CABBAGE, ORANGE & RADISH SALAD

prep & cook time **25 minutes** serves **4**
nutritional count per serving **9.3g total fat**
(1.3g saturated fat); 472kJ (113 cal);
5g carbohydrate; 1.3g protein; 2.9g fibre

1 medium orange (240g)
2 cups (160g) finely shredded white cabbage
2 red radishes (70g), trimmed, sliced thinly
½ cup loosely packed fresh mint leaves
cumin and orange dressing
1 teaspoon cumin seeds
¼ teaspoon hot paprika
2 tablespoons olive oil
1 tablespoon white balsamic vinegar

1 Segment orange over small bowl; reserve
1 tablespoon juice for dressing.
2 Make cumin and orange dressing.
3 Combine orange segments, dressing and
remaining ingredients in large bowl.
cumin and orange dressing Dry-fry spices
in heated small frying pan until fragrant; cool.
Combine spices with oil, vinegar and reserved
orange juice in screw-top jar; shake well.

warm red cabbage & bacon salad

german potato salad

GERMAN POTATO SALAD

prep & cook time **30 minutes** serves **8**
nutritional count per serving **11.3g total fat**
(2.6g saturated fat); 915kJ (219 cal);
18g carbohydrate; 9.8g protein; 3.1g fibre

1kg potatoes, unpeeled, cut into 2cm cubes
4 rindless bacon rashers (260g), sliced thinly
1 medium red onion (170g), sliced thinly
1 teaspoon black mustard seeds
⅔ cup finely chopped fresh flat-leaf parsley
sweet dijon dressing
¼ cup (60ml) cider vinegar
¼ cup (60ml) olive oil
1 tablespoon dijon mustard
½ teaspoon caster sugar

1 Boil, steam or microwave potato until
tender; drain.
2 Meanwhile, make sweet dijon dressing.
3 Cook bacon in heated medium frying pan
until crisp; drain on absorbent paper. Cook
onion in same pan, stirring, until softened.
Add mustard seeds; cook, stirring, 1 minute.
4 Combine potato, bacon, onion mixture,
parsley and dressing in large bowl.
sweet dijon dressing Combine ingredients
in screw-top jar; shake well.

note We used red-skinned potatoes in this recipe.

sumac, onion & mint salad

SUMAC, ONION & MINT SALAD

prep time **10 minutes** serves **8**
nutritional count per serving **4.6g total fat**
(0.6g saturated fat); 238kJ (57 cal);
2.8g carbohydrate; 0.7g protein; 0.7g fibre

4 small red onions (400g), sliced thinly
2 tablespoons olive oil
2 tablespoons finely chopped fresh mint
1 tablespoon lemon juice
1 tablespoon sumac

1 Combine ingredients in medium bowl.

black bean and mango salad

FOUR BEAN SALAD

prep & cook time **1 hour (+ standing)** serves 8
nutritional count per serving **9.6g total fat**
(1.4g saturated fat); 681kJ (163 cal);
11.4g carbohydrate; 5.6g protein; 4.5g fibre

¼ cup (45g) dried lima beans
¼ cup (50g) dried borlotti beans
¼ cup (50g) dried kidney beans
¼ cup (50g) dried cannellini beans
125g cherry tomatoes, halved
½ small red onion (50g), sliced thinly
½ small green capsicum (75g), sliced thinly
½ cup loosely packed fresh flat-leaf
   parsley leaves
wholegrain mustard dressing
⅓ cup (80ml) olive oil
2 tablespoons red wine vinegar
2 teaspoons wholegrain mustard

1 Cover lima beans with cold water in medium bowl. Cover remaining beans with cold water in another medium bowl. Stand beans overnight; rinse, drain.
2 Cook beans, separately, in medium saucepans of boiling water until tender; drain.
3 Make wholegrain mustard dressing.
4 Combine beans, dressing and remaining ingredients in medium bowl.
wholegrain mustard dressing Combine ingredients in screw-top jar; shake well.

BLACK BEAN AND MANGO SALAD

prep & cook time **1 hour 40 minutes**
(+ standing) serves 6
nutritional count per serving **9.9g total fat**
(1.5g saturated fat); 790kJ (189 cal);
9.7g carbohydrate; 11.6g protein; 7.8g fibre

1 cup (200g) dried black beans
1 lebanese cucumber (130g), seeded,
   sliced thinly
1 medium mango (430g), chopped finely
1 cup loosely packed fresh coriander leaves
sweet chilli dressing
1 tablespoon peanut oil
1 tablespoon sweet chilli sauce
1 tablespoon lime juice

1 Cover beans with cold water in medium bowl. Stand overnight; rinse, drain.
2 Cook beans in medium saucepan of boiling water until tender; drain.
3 Meanwhile, make sweet chilli dressing.
4 Combine beans, dressing and remaining ingredients in medium bowl.
sweet chilli dressing Combine ingredients in screw-top jar; shake well.

four bean salad

grilled mushroom, tomato & basil salad

GRILLED MUSHROOM, TOMATO & BASIL SALAD

prep & cook time **20 minutes** serves **4**
nutritional count per serving **23.2g total fat**
(3.2g saturated fat); 1028kJ (246 cal);
3.4g carbohydrate; 4.6g protein; 4.3g fibre

4 flat mushrooms (320g)
4 medium tomatoes (600g), seeded,
   chopped finely
2 tablespoons olive oil
2 teaspoons balsamic vinegar
2 cloves garlic, crushed
1 cup loosely packed fresh basil leaves,
   shredded finely
balsamic vinaigrette
¼ cup (60ml) olive oil
1 tablespoon balsamic vinegar

1 Combine mushrooms, tomato, oil, vinegar
and garlic in medium bowl.
2 Cook mushrooms and tomato on heated
oiled grill plate (or grill or barbecue) until browned
lightly and heated through.
3 Meanwhile, make balsamic vinaigrette.
4 Divide mushrooms among plates; top with
tomato and basil, drizzle with vinaigrette.
balsamic vinaigrette Combine ingredients
in screw-top jar; shake well.

roasted mixed tomato salad

ROASTED MIXED TOMATO SALAD

prep & cook time **20 minutes (+ cooling)** serves **10**
nutritional count per serving **3.8g total fat**
(0.5g saturated fat); 209kJ (50 cal);
2.4g carbohydrate; 1g protein; 1.6g fibre

4 small red tomatoes (360g), halved
4 small green tomatoes (360g), halved
250g cherry tomatoes
200g red teardrop tomatoes
200g yellow teardrop tomatoes
2 tablespoons olive oil
2 tablespoons balsamic vinegar
2 tablespoons small fresh basil leaves
1 tablespoon fresh oregano leaves
1 tablespoon fresh thyme leaves

1 Preheat oven to 240°C/220°C fan-forced.
2 Combine tomatoes and oil in large shallow
baking dish. Roast, uncovered, 10 minutes.
Remove from oven; cool 30 minutes.
3 Combine tomato mixture and remaining
ingredients in large bowl.
serve with **grissini (breadsticks)**.

tomato & herb salad with toasted lavash

TOMATO & HERB SALAD WITH TOASTED LAVASH

prep & cook time **15 minutes (+ refrigeration)** serves **4**
nutritional count per serving **14.5g total fat
(2g saturated fat); 957kJ (229 cal);
17.4g carbohydrate; 4.7g protein; 5.9g fibre**

¼ cup (40g) burghul
2 tablespoons lemon juice
1 piece lavash bread (60g), cut into wedges
2 cups loosely packed fresh flat-leaf
    parsley leaves
1 cup coarsely chopped fresh mint
2 green onions, sliced thinly
¼ cup (60ml) olive oil
4 medium tomatoes (450g), cut into
    1cm thick slices

1 Combine burghul and juice in small bowl;
refrigerate 1 hour.
2 Meanwhile, preheat oven to 180°C/160°C
fan-forced. Place bread on oven tray; bake
about 5 minutes or until crisp.
3 Combine burghul mixture with parsley, mint,
onion and oil in medium bowl.
4 Stack tomatoes with burghul mixture on
serving plates; accompany with bread pieces.

BABY COS CAESAR SALAD

prep & cook time **30 minutes** serves **4**
nutritional count per serving **54.2g total fat
(11.5g saturated fat); 2809kJ (672 cal);
22.2g carbohydrate; 23.6g protein; 3.5g fibre**

1 small french bread stick (150g), sliced thinly
¼ cup (60ml) olive oil
4 slices prosciutto (60g)
4 eggs
2 baby cos lettuce (360g), leaves separated
1 cup (80g) flaked parmesan cheese
caesar dressing
2 egg yolks
1 clove garlic, quartered
4 drained anchovy fillets
2 tablespoons lemon juice
2 teaspoons dijon mustard
½ cup (125ml) olive oil
1 tablespoon warm water, approximately

1 Preheat oven to 180°C/160°C fan-forced.
2 Make caesar dressing.
3 Combine bread and oil in medium bowl.
Place bread, in single layer, on oven tray; toast,
in oven, until croûtons are browned lightly.
4 Meanwhile, cook prosciutto in heated large
frying pan until crisp; drain on absorbent paper,
chop coarsely.
5 Poach eggs until the whites are set but the
yolks are still runny.
6 Combine lettuce, cheese, croûtons,
prosciutto and dressing in large bowl; divide
among serving bowls. Serve topped with
poached eggs.
caesar dressing Blend or process egg yolks,
garlic, anchovies, juice and mustard until
smooth. With motor operating, gradually add
oil in a thin steady stream; blend until dressing
thickens. Add as much of the warm water as
required to thin dressing.

baby cos caesar salad

CRISPY SNOW PEA, PRAWN AND AVOCADO SALAD

prep & cook time 25 minutes   **serves** 4
nutritional count per serving 38.2g total fat
(7.2g saturated fat); 1998kJ (478 cal);
8.2g carbohydrate; 24.6g protein; 3.7g fibre

750g cooked medium king prawns
150g sugar snap peas, trimmed
3 small avocados (600g), sliced thickly
2 cups (100g) snow pea sprouts
chive vinaigrette
¼ cup (60ml) white wine vinegar
¼ cup (60ml) olive oil
¼ cup finely chopped fresh chives

1 Make chive vinaigrette.
2 Shell and devein prawns leaving tails intact.
3 Boil, steam or microwave peas until just
tender; rinse under cold water, drain.
4 Combine peas in large bowl with prawns,
avocado, sprouts and vinaigrette; toss gently.
chive vinaigrette Combine ingredients in
screw-top jar; shake well.

SEAFOOD
SALADS

prawn, pink grapefruit and fetta salad

SALAD NIÇOISE

prep & cook time **20 minutes** serves **4**
nutritional count per serving **16.9g total fat**
(3.7g saturated fat); 1522kJ (364 cal);
19.5g carbohydrate; 30.9g protein; 5.2g fibre

200g baby green beans, trimmed
2 tablespoons olive oil
1 tablespoon lemon juice
2 tablespoons white wine vinegar
4 medium tomatoes (600g), cut into wedges
4 hard-boiled eggs, quartered
425g can tuna in springwater, drained, flaked
½ cup (80g) drained caperberries, rinsed
½ cup (60g) seeded small black olives
¼ cup firmly packed fresh flat-leaf
    parsley leaves
440g can drained whole baby new potatoes,
    rinsed, halved

1 Boil, steam or microwave beans until tender;
drain. Rinse under cold water; drain.
2 Whisk oil, juice and vinegar in large bowl; add
beans and remaining ingredients, toss gently.

PRAWN, PINK GRAPEFRUIT AND FETTA SALAD

prep time **30 minutes** serves **8**
nutritional count per serving **17.9g total fat**
(6.5g saturated fat); 1346kJ (322 cal);
5.1g carbohydrate; 34.5g protein; 1.2g fibre

24 cooked large king prawns (1.6kg)
1 baby cos lettuce (180g), trimmed,
    leaves separated
2 small pink grapefruit (700g), segmented
200g fetta cheese, crumbled
chilli mint dressing
¼ cup (60ml) olive oil
¼ cup (60ml) red wine vinegar
1 teaspoon white sugar
¼ cup coarsely chopped fresh mint
1 fresh long red chilli, sliced thinly

1 Shell and devein prawns leaving tails intact.
2 Make chilli mint dressing.
3 Divide lettuce, prawns, grapefruit and
cheese among serving plates; drizzle with
chilli mint dressing.
chilli mint dressing Combine ingredients in
screw-top jar; shake well.

salad niçoise

poached trout and potato salad

POACHED TROUT AND POTATO SALAD

prep & cook time **25 minutes** serves **4**
nutritional count per serving **24.3g total fat**
(3.9g saturated fat); 2031kJ (486 cal);
29.3g carbohydrate; 34.9g protein; 5.1g fibre

800g small kipfler potatoes, unpeeled,
halved lengthways
1 litre (4 cups) water
4 x 5cm strips lemon rind
2 sprigs fresh dill
600g ocean trout fillets
1 small red onion (100g), sliced thinly
1 lebanese cucumber (130g), seeded,
sliced thinly
50g rocket leaves
lemon and dill dressing
⅓ cup (80ml) olive oil
¼ cup (60ml) lemon juice
1 clove garlic, crushed
1 tablespoon finely chopped fresh dill
1 tablespoon rinsed, drained baby capers

1 Boil, steam or microwave potato until
tender; drain.
2 Combine the water, rind and dill in medium
saucepan; bring to the boil. Add fish; simmer,
covered, about 10 minutes or until cooked as
desired. Drain fish; discard cooking liquid. Flake
fish coarsely into large bowl; discard skin.
3 Meanwhile, make lemon and dill dressing.
4 Add potato, remaining ingredients and
dressing to bowl with fish; toss gently.
lemon and dill dressing Combine ingredients
in screw-top jar; shake well.

ruby red grapefruit, salmon and mizuna salad

RUBY RED GRAPEFRUIT, SALMON AND MIZUNA SALAD

prep time **15 minutes** serves **4**
nutritional count per serving **19.1g total fat**
(3g saturated fat); 1229kJ (294 cal);
8.6g carbohydrate; 21.1g protein; 2.4g fibre

300g sliced smoked salmon
2 ruby red grapefruit (700g)
2 tablespoons olive oil
1 teaspoon dijon mustard
150g mizuna
⅓ cup (50g) roasted cashews,
chopped coarsely
½ small red onion (50g), sliced thinly

1 Reserve four slices of salmon; cut remaining
slices into thick pieces.
2 Segment grapefruit over large bowl; add oil,
mustard, mizuna, nuts, onion and fish pieces,
mix gently.
3 Divide salad among serving plates; top with
reserved salmon slices.

crab and green mango salad

SMOKED SALMON, ORANGE & AVOCADO SALAD

prep time **15 minutes** serves **4**
nutritional count per serving **35.9g total fat**
(7.7g saturated fat); 1856kJ (444 cal);
10.9g carbohydrate; 18.3g protein; 4.3g fibre

2 large oranges (600g), segmented
2 large avocados (640g), halved, sliced
    thickly
2 x 150g smoked salmon portions,
    skinned, flaked
40g baby spinach leaves
10g trimmed lambs lettuce
horseradish cream dressing
¼ cup (60ml) orange juice
1 tablespoon olive oil
1 tablespoon white wine vinegar
1 tablespoon horseradish cream

1 Make horseradish cream dressing.
2 Combine orange, avocado, fish, spinach
and lettuce in large bowl. Divide salad among
serving plates; drizzle with dressing.
horseradish cream dressing Combine
ingredients in screw-top jar; shake well.

notes You need about two punnets of untrimmed
lambs lettuce for this recipe.
You can use smoked ocean trout portions instead
of the salmon.

CRAB AND GREEN MANGO SALAD

prep & cook time **20 minutes** serves **4**
nutritional count per serving **1.4g total fat**
(0.1g saturated fat); 953kJ (228 cal);
37.2g carbohydrate; 14g protein; 3.9g fibre

125g bean thread noodles
2 green mangoes (700g), cut into
    matchsticks
300g cooked crab meat, flaked
1 small red onion (100g), sliced thinly
100g baby mizuna leaves
1 cup firmly packed fresh coriander leaves
sweet chilli dressing
⅓ cup (80ml) lime juice
2 tablespoons fish sauce
2 tablespoons sweet chilli sauce
1 tablespoon grated palm sugar

1 Place noodles in medium heatproof bowl,
cover with boiling water; stand until almost
tender, drain. Rinse under cold water; drain.
2 Meanwhile, make sweet chilli dressing.
3 Combine noodles and dressing in large bowl
with remaining ingredients.
sweet chilli dressing Combine ingredients in
screw-top jar; shake well.

smoked salmon, orange & avocado salad

tamarind and chilli octopus salad

TAMARIND AND CHILLI OCTOPUS SALAD

prep & cook time 35 minutes serves 4
nutritional count per serving 24.7g total fat
(4.1g saturated fat); 1806kJ (432 cal);
7.6g carbohydrate; 43.9g protein; 2.5g fibre

1kg cleaned baby octopus
1 tablespoon tamarind concentrate
1 fresh small red thai chilli, chopped finely
2 tablespoons peanut oil
1 cup (80g) bean sprouts
1 cup (50g) snow pea sprouts
100g snow peas, trimmed, sliced thinly
    lengthways
1 small red capsicum (150g), sliced thinly
1 cup loosely packed fresh coriander leaves
lime and palm sugar dressing
¼ cup (60ml) peanut oil
1 teaspoon finely grated lime rind
2 tablespoons lime juice
1 tablespoon grated palm sugar

1 Make lime and palm sugar dressing.
2 Combine octopus, tamarind, chilli and half
the oil in large bowl.
3 Heat remaining oil in wok; stir-fry octopus, in
batches, until cooked.
4 Combine octopus, dressing and remaining
ingredients in large bowl.
lime and palm sugar dressing Combine
ingredients in screw-top jar; shake well.

TUNA SALAD

prep time 15 minutes serves 4
nutritional count per serving 26.1g total fat
(4.9g saturated fat); 1492kJ (357 cal);
4.6g carbohydrate; 24.4g protein; 4.9g fibre

¼ cup (60ml) olive oil
2 tablespoons white wine vinegar
1 tablespoon lemon juice
2 teaspoons finely chopped fresh basil
2 teaspoons finely chopped fresh oregano
1 clove garlic, crushed
1 fresh long red chilli, chopped finely
1 medium iceberg lettuce, cut into wedges
425g can tuna in springwater, drained, flaked

tuna salad

250g cherry tomatoes, halved
1 medium avocado (250g), chopped coarsely
1 lebanese cucumber (130g), sliced thinly
1 small red onion (100g), sliced thinly

1 Combine oil, vinegar, juice, herbs, garlic and
chilli in screw-top jar; shake well.
2 Place lettuce wedges on serving plate; top
with remaining ingredients. Drizzle with dressing.

note Salmon can be substituted for the tuna.

SMOKED CHICKEN, SPINACH AND ALMOND SALAD

prep & cook time 30 minutes **serves** 4
nutritional count per serving 33.5g total fat
(5.3g saturated fat); 2044kJ (489 cal);
11.3g carbohydrate; 34g protein; 4.7g fibre

350g smoked chicken breast fillets,
 sliced thinly
3 stalks celery (450g), trimmed, sliced thinly
3 small tomatoes (270g), quartered, seeded
100g baby spinach leaves
4 hard-boiled eggs, quartered
2 green onions, sliced thinly
½ cup (70g) slivered almonds, roasted
cumin mayonnaise
2 teaspoons cumin seeds, toasted
½ cup (150g) mayonnaise
¼ cup (60ml) lemon juice

1 Make cumin mayonnaise.
2 Combine chicken, celery, tomato, spinach,
egg, onion and nuts in large bowl.
3 Divide salad among serving plates; drizzle
over mayonnaise.
cumin mayonnaise Using mortar and pestle,
crush seeds finely; combine with mayonnaise
and juice in small bowl.

chicken, preserved lemon and cranberry rice salad

CHICKEN, PRESERVED LEMON AND CRANBERRY RICE SALAD

prep & cook time **25 minutes** serves 4
nutritional count per serving **27.1g total fat**
(5.2g saturated fat); 2646kJ (633 cal);
59.3g carbohydrate; 36.3g protein; 3.2g fibre

2 cups (500ml) water
4 x 5cm strips lemon rind
600g chicken breast fillets
3 cups cooked wild rice blend
1 cup thinly sliced fresh mint
½ cup (65g) dried cranberries
2 tablespoons finely chopped
    preserved lemon rind
lemon cranberry dressing
⅓ cup (80ml) olive oil
¼ cup (60ml) cranberry juice
2 tablespoons lemon juice
2 teaspoons caster sugar
1 tablespoon cranberry sauce

1 Combine the water and rind in medium
saucepan; bring to the boil. Add chicken;
simmer, covered, about 10 minutes or until
chicken is cooked through. Cool chicken in
liquid 10 minutes; drain. Slice chicken thinly.

2 Meanwhile, make lemon cranberry dressing.
3 Combine chicken, dressing and remaining
ingredients in large bowl.
lemon cranberry dressing Combine
ingredients in screw-top jar; shake well.

SMOKED CHICKEN, PEACH & PECAN SALAD

prep & cook time **20 minutes** serves 4
nutritional count per serving **50.5g total fat**
(6.9g saturated fat); 2750kJ (658 cal);
7.4g carbohydrate; 42.4g protein; 5.2g fibre

170g asparagus, trimmed, cut into
    3cm lengths
600g smoked chicken breast fillets,
    sliced thinly
1 small red onion (100g), sliced thinly
2 medium peaches (300g), sliced thinly
1 cup (120g) roasted pecans
150g baby spinach leaves
dill vinaigrette
⅓ cup (80ml) olive oil
2 tablespoons cider vinegar
1 tablespoon finely chopped fresh dill

1 Boil, steam or microwave asparagus until
tender; drain. Rinse under cold water; drain.
2 Make dill vinaigrette.
3 Combine asparagus and vinaigrette with
remaining ingredients in large bowl.
dill vinaigrette Combine ingredients in screw-
top jar; shake well.

smoked chicken, peach & pecan salad

chilli lime chicken salad

CHILLI LIME CHICKEN SALAD

prep & cook time **30 minutes** serves **4**
nutritional count per serving **27.2g total fat**
(4.2g saturated fat); 2157kJ (516 cal);
21.5g carbohydrate; 47g protein; 4g fibre

2 cups (500ml) water
2 cups (500ml) chicken stock
4 single chicken breasts fillets (680g)
1 small red capsicum (150g), sliced thinly
4 trimmed red radishes (60g), sliced thinly
¼ small wombok (175g), shredded coarsely
3 green onions, sliced thinly
1 cup (80g) bean sprouts
½ cup loosely packed fresh coriander leaves
½ cup (75g) roasted salted peanuts
chilli lime dressing
⅓ cup (80ml) lime juice
¼ cup (65g) grated palm sugar
2 fresh small red thai chillies, chopped finely
1 clove garlic, crushed
1 tablespoon fish sauce
¼ cup (60ml) peanut oil

1 Bring the water and stock to the boil in large frying pan. Add chicken, reduce heat; simmer, covered, about 10 minutes or until cooked through. Remove from heat; cool chicken in liquid 10 minutes. Slice chicken thinly.
2 Meanwhile, make chilli lime dressing.
3 Place remaining ingredients and half the dressing in large bowl; toss gently.
4 Divide salad among serving plates; top with chicken, drizzle with remaining dressing.
chilli lime dressing Combine juice, sugar, chilli and garlic in small saucepan. Stir over low heat until sugar dissolves; cool 10 minutes. Whisk in sauce and oil.

smoked chicken and dried cranberry salad

SMOKED CHICKEN AND DRIED CRANBERRY SALAD

prep time **15 minutes** serves **4**
nutritional count per serving **39.8g total fat**
(5.2g saturated fat); 2420kJ (579 cal);
17.7g carbohydrate; 35.5g protein; 5.9g fibre

2 teaspoons dijon mustard
¼ cup (60ml) cider vinegar
2 tablespoons olive oil
500g smoked chicken breast fillets,
    sliced thinly
1 large green apple (200g), unpeeled,
    sliced thinly
1 cup (120g) roasted pecans
½ cup (65g) dried cranberries
150g baby spinach leaves
1 cup loosely packed fresh flat-leaf
    parsley leaves

1 Combine mustard, vinegar and oil in screw-top jar; shake well.
2 Combine dressing with remaining ingredients in large bowl.

chicken & rocket pesto pasta salad

rocket pesto Blend or process rocket, nuts, cheese, rind and juice until finely chopped. With motor operating, gradually add oil in a thin steady stream; blend until pesto is smooth.

note **You need one large barbecued chicken, weighing approximately 900g, for this recipe.**

CREAMY CHICKEN AND PASTA SALAD

prep & cook time **35 minutes** serves **6**
nutritional count per serving **39.1g total fat (8.8g saturated fat); 3097kJ (741 cal); 67.5g carbohydrate; 27.1g protein; 5.7g fibre**

3 cups (750ml) water
400g chicken breast fillets
500g large pasta shells
2 stalks celery (300g), trimmed, sliced thinly
1 small red onion (100g), sliced thinly
1 cup (120g) roasted pecans
½ cup (90g) thinly sliced cornichons
50g baby rocket leaves
creamy tarragon dressing
¾ cup (225g) mayonnaise
½ cup (120g) sour cream
2 tablespoons lemon juice
1 tablespoon finely chopped fresh tarragon

1 Bring the water to the boil in medium saucepan, add chicken; reduce heat, simmer, covered, about 10 minutes. Cool chicken in poaching liquid 10 minutes; drain, slice thinly.
2 Meanwhile, cook pasta in large saucepan of boiling water until tender; drain. Rinse under cold water; drain.
3 Make creamy tarragon dressing.
4 Combine pasta in large bowl with chicken, dressing and remaining ingredients.
creamy tarragon dressing Combine ingredients in small bowl.

note **Cornichon, French for gherkin, is a very small variety of pickled cucumber. They are available from major supermarkets.**

CHICKEN & ROCKET PESTO PASTA SALAD

prep & cook time **30 minutes** serves **4**
nutritional count per serving **32.4g total fat (7.1g saturated fat); 3168kJ (758 cal); 66.6g carbohydrate; 47g protein; 5.6g fibre**

375g large shell pasta
1 cup (120g) frozen peas
3 cups (480g) shredded barbecued chicken
40g baby rocket leaves
rocket pesto
40g baby rocket leaves
2 tablespoons pine nuts, roasted
½ cup (40g) finely grated parmesan cheese
2 teaspoons finely grated lemon rind
1 tablespoon lemon juice
¼ cup (60ml) olive oil

1 Cook pasta in large saucepan of boiling water until tender. Add peas during last 2 minutes of pasta cooking time; drain.
2 Meanwhile, make rocket pesto.
3 Combine pasta, peas and rocket pesto in large bowl with remaining ingredients.

creamy chicken and pasta salad

THAI CHICKEN AND LYCHEE SALAD

prep time **25 minutes** serves **4**

Combine 3 cups shredded barbecued chicken, 565g can drained, halved, seeded lychees in syrup, 1 thinly sliced small red onion, 8 thinly sliced green onions, 2 cups bean sprouts, ½ cup firmly packed fresh mint leaves and ½ cup firmly packed fresh coriander leaves in large bowl. Combine 1 teaspoon finely grated lime rind, 1 teaspoon sambal oelek, ¼ cup lime juice, 1 teaspoon sesame oil, 1 tablespoon brown sugar and 2 teaspoons fish sauce in screw-top jar; shake well. Drizzle dressing over salad; toss gently to combine.

CHICKEN SALAD WITH SESAME DRESSING

prep time **20 minutes** serves **4**

Cut 1 large barbecued chicken into 8 pieces; place in large bowl. Using a vegetable peeler, peel thin strips lengthways from 2 medium carrots. Combine carrot with ½ thickly shredded small wombok, 6 thickly sliced green onions, 1 cup bean sprouts and ¼ cup firmly packed fresh coriander leaves in large bowl with chicken. Combine 2 crushed garlic cloves, 2 tablespoons peanut oil, 1 tablespoon soy sauce, ½ teaspoon sesame oil, 1 tablespoon lemon juice, 1 teaspoon white sugar and 1 tablespoon white wine vinegar in screw-top jar; shake well. Drizzle dressing over salad.

BBQ CHICKEN SALADS

CHICKEN CAESAR SALAD

prep & cook time **20 minutes** serves **4**

Toss together 1 sliced cos lettuce, 3 rashers coarsely chopped cooked bacon, 3 cups shredded barbecued chicken, 4 quartered hard-boiled eggs, ½ cup shaved parmesan cheese and ½ cup caesar dressing.

CHICKEN PASTA SALAD

prep & cook time **25 minutes** serves **4**

Combine 4 cups cooked penne pasta with 150g crumbled fetta cheese, 150g coarsely chopped char-grilled capsicum, 3 cups coarsely chopped barbecued chicken, ⅓ cup roasted coarsely chopped walnuts, 1 cup basil leaves and ½ cup italian dressing.

crispy duck and fig salad with spiced balsamic glaze

CRISPY DUCK AND FIG SALAD WITH SPICED BALSAMIC GLAZE

prep & cook time **25 minutes** serves **4**
nutritional count per serving **55.6g total fat**
(16.7g saturated fat); 2650kJ (634 cal);
12.6g carbohydrate; 21g protein; 2.9g fibre

600g duck breast fillets, skin on
80g trimmed watercress
250g yellow grape tomatoes, halved
4 medium figs (240g), cut into wedges
spiced balsamic glaze
½ cup (125ml) balsamic vinegar
2 tablespoons brown sugar
½ teaspoon ground cinnamon
¼ teaspoon ground cloves

1 Make spiced balsamic glaze.
2 Meanwhile, cook duck, skin-side down, in heated oiled large frying pan about 5 minutes or until skin is crisp. Turn duck; cook about 5 minutes or until cooked as desired. Cover, stand 5 minutes then slice duck thinly.
3 Place watercress and tomato in medium bowl with dressing; toss gently. Divide figs among plates; top with tomato mixture then duck.
spiced balsamic glaze Combine ingredients in small saucepan; stir over low heat, without boiling, until sugar dissolves. Bring to the boil; simmer, uncovered, about 5 minutes or until syrup thickens slightly. Cool.

note If glaze becomes too thick, stir in a little boiling water.

CHICKEN, GRILLED VEGETABLES AND HALOUMI SALAD

prep & cook time **50 minutes** serves **4**
nutritional count per serving **49.1g total fat**
(17.2g saturated fat); 3106kJ (743 cal);
12.2g carbohydrate; 62.6g protein; 3.8g fibre

2 tablespoons olive oil
1 tablespoon balsamic vinegar
2 cloves garlic, crushed
1 tablespoon coarsely chopped fresh
    rosemary leaves
800g chicken thigh fillets
600g piece pumpkin, trimmed, sliced thinly

chicken, grilled vegetables and haloumi salad

300g asparagus, trimmed
2 x 180g packets haloumi cheese
250g rocket, trimmed
rosemary balsamic dressing
2 tablespoons olive oil
1 tablespoon balsamic vinegar
1 tablespoon lemon juice
1 tablespoon coarsely chopped fresh
    rosemary leaves

1 Make rosemary balsamic dressing.
2 Combine oil, vinegar, garlic, rosemary and chicken in medium bowl. Cook chicken on heated oiled grill plate (or grill or barbecue) until cooked as desired; cover.
3 Cook pumpkin and asparagus, in batches, on grill plate until tender. Transfer to large bowl; cover.
4 Slice cheese thickly; cook on cleaned grill plate until browned both sides.
5 Slice chicken thickly. Combine with cheese, rocket and dressing in bowl with pumpkin and asparagus; toss gently.
rosemary balsamic dressing Combine ingredients in screw-top jar; shake well.

FATTOUSH WITH HARISSA-RUBBED LAMB

prep & cook time 45 minutes
(+ refrigeration) **serves** 4
nutritional count per serving 28.9g total fat
(8.2g saturated fat); 2416kJ (578 cal);
36.7g carbohydrate; 39.6g protein; 6.4g fibre

600g lamb backstraps
¼ cup (75g) harissa paste
¼ cup (60ml) olive oil
3 pocket pitta breads (255g)
3 medium tomatoes (450g), cut into wedges
1 large green capsicum (350g), sliced thickly
2 lebanese cucumbers (260g), halved,
    sliced thinly
½ cup coarsely chopped fresh mint
1 cup firmly packed fresh flat-leaf
    parsley leaves
¼ cup (60ml) lemon juice
1 clove garlic, crushed

1 Combine lamb and harissa in medium bowl;
rub harissa into lamb. Refrigerate 1 hour.
2 Heat 1 tablespoon of the oil in large frying
pan; cook lamb to your liking. Cover; stand
5 minutes then slice thickly.
3 Preheat grill. Split pittas in half; grill both
sides until browned lightly.
4 Combine remaining ingredients in large bowl;
break pitta into pieces over salad. Serve
fattoush topped with lamb.

MEAT
SALADS

lamb and fetta salad with
warm walnut dressing

LAMB AND FETTA SALAD WITH WARM WALNUT DRESSING

prep & cook time **25 minutes** serves **4**
nutritional count per serving 52.8g total fat
(16.8g saturated fat); 2742kJ (656 cal);
1.2g carbohydrate; 43.8g protein; 3.2g fibre

1 tablespoon vegetable oil
600g lamb fillets
200g fetta cheese, crumbled
250g witlof, trimmed, leaves separated
150g baby spinach leaves, trimmed
warm walnut dressing
2 cloves garlic, crushed
1 teaspoon finely grated lemon rind
¼ cup (60ml) olive oil
2 tablespoons cider vinegar
½ cup (55g) coarsely chopped
   roasted walnuts

1 Heat oil in large frying pan; cook lamb until cooked as desired. Cover; stand 5 minutes then slice thickly.
2 Make warm walnut dressing.
3 Combine lamb in medium bowl with remaining ingredients. Serve salad drizzled with dressing.

warm walnut dressing Cook garlic, rind, oil and vinegar in small pan, stirring, until hot. Remove from heat; stir in nuts.

PEPPERED LAMB WITH PEA, MINT AND WATERCRESS SALAD

prep & cook time **30 minutes** serves **4**
nutritional count per serving 31.1g total fat
(12g saturated fat); 2006kJ (480 cal);
5.1g carbohydrate; 43.2g protein; 5g fibre

2 tablespoons mixed peppercorns
1 tablespoon olive oil
600g lamb fillets
1 cup (160g) fresh or frozen peas
250g yellow teardrop tomatoes, halved
100g watercress, trimmed
200g fetta cheese, cut into batons
¼ cup coarsely chopped fresh mint
white wine vinaigrette
¼ cup (60ml) white wine vinegar
1 tablespoon olive oil
1 clove garlic, crushed

1 Using mortar and pestle, crush peppercorns until ground coarsely. Combine peppercorns, oil and lamb in medium bowl. Cook lamb in heated oiled large frying pan until cooked as desired. Cover lamb; stand 5 minutes then slice thinly.
2 Meanwhile, make white wine vinaigrette.
3 Boil, steam or microwave peas until tender; drain. Rinse under cold water; drain.
4 Combine lamb, peas, vinaigrette and remaining ingredients in large bowl.
white wine vinaigrette Combine ingredients in screw-top jar; shake well.

peppered lamb with pea, mint and watercress salad

turkish lamb and yogurt salad

TURKISH LAMB AND YOGURT SALAD

prep & cook time **25 minutes** serves **4**
nutritional count per serving **10.8g** total fat
(3.4g saturated fat); 1062kJ (254 cal);
5.1g carbohydrate; 32.9g protein; 2.7g fibre

600g lamb backstraps
2 tablespoons sumac
1 tablespoon olive oil
¼ cup (70g) yogurt
2 tablespoons lemon juice
250g cherry tomatoes, halved
2 lebanese cucumbers (260g), seeded,
**   sliced thinly**
½ cup loosely packed fresh flat-leaf
**   parsley leaves**
½ cup loosely packed fresh mint leaves
1 small red onion (100g), sliced thinly

1 Rub lamb with sumac. Heat oil in large
frying pan; cook lamb, uncovered, until
cooked as desired. Cover lamb; stand
5 minutes then slice thinly.
2 Meanwhile, whisk yogurt and juice in
small jug.
3 Combine lamb and remaining ingredients
in large bowl; drizzle with dressing.

BEETROOT SALAD WITH HONEY BALSAMIC LAMB

prep & cook time **40 minutes**
(+ refrigeration) serves **4**
nutritional count per serving **28.9g** total fat
(9.1g saturated fat); 2228kJ (533 cal);
19.2g carbohydrate; 47.9g protein; 2.8g fibre

800g lamb fillets
1 tablespoon honey
1 tablespoon balsamic vinegar
1 clove garlic, crushed
500g fresh baby beetroot, reserve leaves
2 teaspoons olive oil
1 lebanese cucumber (130g), seeded,
**   sliced thinly**
200g ricotta cheese, crumbled
honey balsamic dressing
¼ cup (60ml) olive oil

beetroot salad with honey balsamic lamb

2 tablespoons balsamic vinegar
1 tablespoon honey
1 teaspoon dijon mustard

1 Combine lamb, honey, vinegar and garlic
in medium bowl; cover, refrigerate 3 hours
or overnight.
2 Preheat oven to 220°C/200°C fan-forced.
3 Remove unblemished leaves from beetroot,
reserve for later use. Peel and quarter beetroot.
Place on oven tray; drizzle with oil. Roast,
uncovered, about 30 minutes or until tender.
4 Meanwhile, cook lamb in heated oiled large
frying pan until cooked as desired. Cover lamb;
stand 5 minutes then slice thinly.
5 Make honey balsamic dressing.
6 Combine lamb, beetroot, beetroot leaves,
cucumber and dressing in large bowl; sprinkle
with cheese.
honey balsamic dressing Combine
ingredients in small bowl.

lamb and red lentil salad

4 Place lentils in large bowl with tomato, celery, onion, coriander and dressing; toss gently to combine.
5 Serve lamb with lentil salad and rocket.
cumin dressing Combine ingredients in screw-top jar; shake well.

MOROCCAN BEEF SALAD

prep & cook time **35 minutes** serves **4**
nutritional count per serving **13.5g total fat**
(4.9g saturated fat); 2834kJ (678 cal);
91.5g carbohydrate; 46.5g protein; 4.4g fibre

1 cup (250ml) vegetable stock
1½ cups (300g) couscous
½ cup (75g) thinly sliced dried apricots
½ cup (80g) sultanas
1 medium red onion (170g), chopped finely
¼ cup finely chopped fresh mint
2 tablespoons coarsely chopped fresh dill
600g beef rump steak
1 tablespoon roasted pine nuts
2 teaspoons cumin seeds
¾ cup (180ml) oil-free french dressing

1 Bring stock to the boil in medium saucepan; remove from heat. Add couscous to stock, cover; stand about 5 minutes or until stock is absorbed, fluffing with fork occasionally. Transfer couscous to large bowl; stir in apricots, sultanas, onion and herbs.
2 Meanwhile, cook beef in heated oiled frying pan until cooked as desired. Cover beef; stand 5 minutes then slice thinly.
3 Place nuts and seeds in small heated frying pan; dry-fry, stirring, until fragrant and nuts are toasted. Place nut mixture in screw-top jar with dressing; shake well.
4 Serve beef on couscous mixture; drizzle with dressing.

LAMB AND RED LENTIL SALAD

prep & cook time **25 minutes** serves **4**
nutritional count per serving **23.6g total fat**
(7.4g saturated fat); 2015kJ (482 cal);
22.9g carbohydrate; 45.4g protein; 9.2g fibre

1 cup (200g) red lentils
600g lamb backstraps
3 medium tomatoes (450g), chopped coarsely
1 stalk celery (150g), trimmed, chopped finely
6 green onions, chopped finely
¼ cup loosely packed fresh coriander leaves
50g rocket leaves
cumin dressing
⅓ cup (80ml) lemon juice
2 tablespoons olive oil
1 teaspoon ground cumin
1 teaspoon sweet paprika

1 Rinse lentils under cold water; drain. Place lentils in medium saucepan, cover with cold water; bring to the boil. Reduce heat; simmer, uncovered, about 5 minutes or until just tender, drain. Rinse under cold water; drain.
2 Cook lamb on heated oiled grill plate (or grill or barbecue) until cooked as desired.
3 Meanwhile, make cumin dressing.

moroccan beef salad

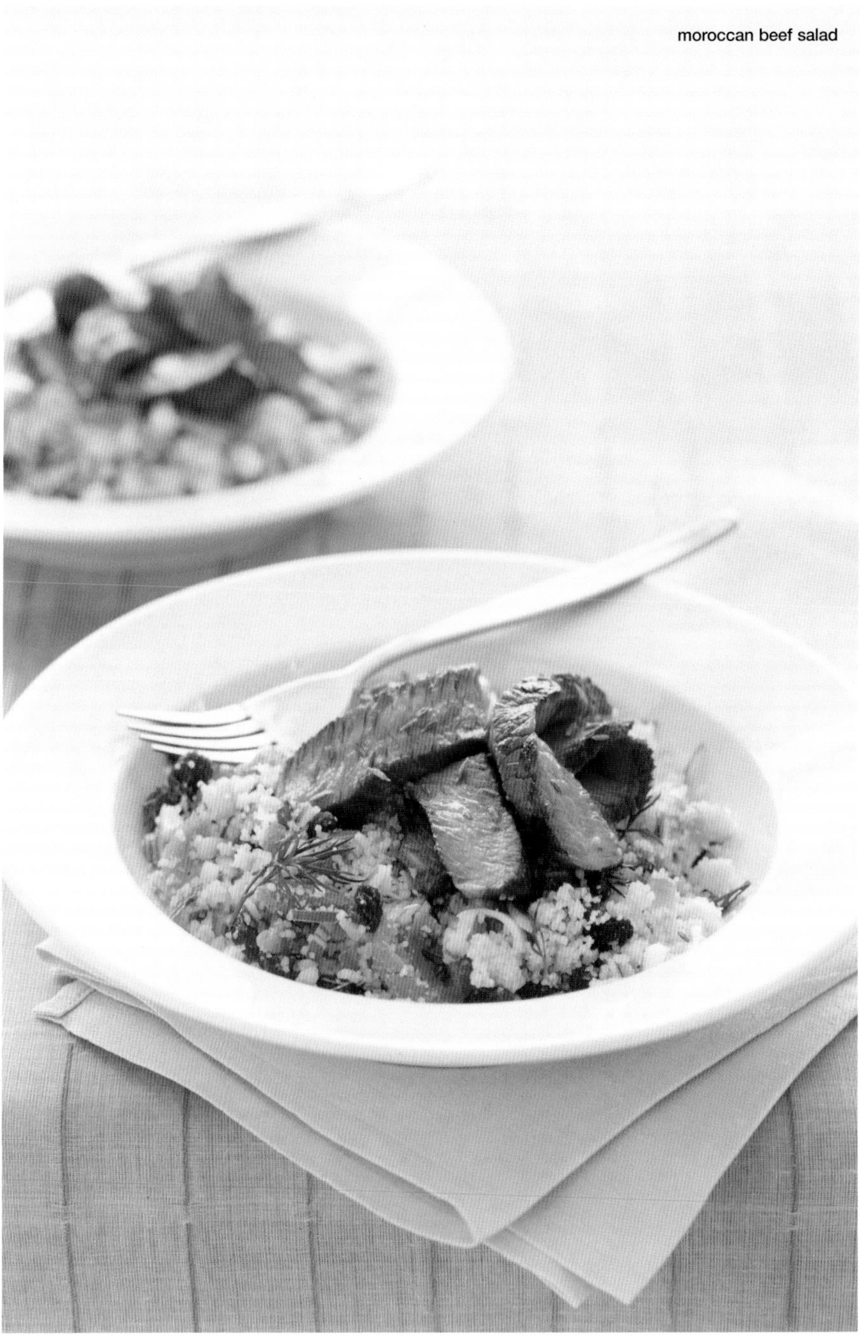

thai beef salad

THAI BEEF SALAD

prep & cook time **25 minutes**
(+ refrigeration) serves **4**
nutritional count per serving **8.8g total fat**
(3.8g saturated fat); 1062kJ (254 cal);
9.6g carbohydrate; 31.4g protein; 4.2g fibre

500g beef rump steak
¼ cup (60ml) fish sauce
¼ cup (60ml) lime juice
1 tablespoon grated palm sugar
2 teaspoons light soy sauce
1 clove garlic, crushed
3 lebanese cucumbers (390g), seeded,
   sliced thinly
4 fresh small red thai chillies, sliced thinly
8 green onions, sliced thinly
250g cherry tomatoes, quartered
1 cup loosely packed vietnamese mint leaves
1 cup loosely packed fresh coriander leaves

1 Combine beef, 2 tablespoons of the fish
sauce and 1 tablespoon of the juice in large
bowl; refrigerate 3 hours or overnight.
2 Drain beef; discard marinade. Cook beef
on heated oiled grill plate (or grill or barbecue).
Cover; stand 5 minutes then slice thinly.
3 Whisk remaining fish sauce and juice with
sugar, soy sauce and garlic in large bowl.
Add beef, cucumber, chilli, onion, tomato
and herbs; toss gently.

CAJUN-SPICED BEEF AND GARLICKY BEAN SALAD

prep & cook time **25 minutes** serves **4**
nutritional count per serving **35.3g total fat**
(8.8g saturated fat); 2445kJ (585 cal);
16.3g carbohydrate; 47.5g protein; 7.5 g fibre

750g piece beef fillet
1 tablespoon cajun spice mix
420g can mixed beans, rinsed, drained
2 lebanese cucumbers (260g), halved
   lengthways, sliced thinly
4 small tomatoes (360g), cut into wedges
1 medium red onion (170g), sliced thinly
1 medium avocado (250g), sliced thickly
½ cup finely chopped fresh coriander

cajun-spiced beef and garlicky bean salad

garlic dressing
¼ cup (60ml) lemon juice
¼ cup (60ml) olive oil
2 cloves garlic, crushed

1 Make garlic dressing.
2 Sprinkle beef both sides with spice mix;
cook on heated oiled grill plate (or grill or
barbecue) until cooked as desired. Cover;
stand 5 minutes then slice thinly.
3 Combine remaining ingredients in large bowl
with dressing; toss gently. Serve salad topped
with beef.
garlic dressing Combine ingredients in
small bowl.

note Cajun spice mix, a blend of ground herbs and
spices that can include basil, paprika, tarragon,
fennel, thyme or cayenne, is available at most
supermarkets and speciality spice shops.

orange, beetroot and rare roast beef salad

ORANGE, BEETROOT AND RARE ROAST BEEF SALAD

prep time **15 minutes** serves **4**
nutritional count per serving **19.9g total fat**
(8.4g saturated fat); 1860kJ (445 cal);
26.8g carbohydrate; 36.4g protein; 6.2g fibre

2 medium oranges (480g)
400g shaved rare roast beef
850g can whole baby beetroot,
    drained, halved
150g baby rocket leaves
½ cup (125ml) buttermilk
¼ cup (75g) mayonnaise
1 tablespoon wholegrain mustard
100g blue cheese, crumbled

1 Segment oranges over large bowl; reserve
1 tablespoon juice separately.
2 Add beef, beetroot and rocket to bowl.
3 Whisk reserved juice, buttermilk, mayonnaise
and mustard in small bowl. Sprinkle cheese over
salad; drizzle with dressing.

BLT SALAD

prep & cook time **25 minutes** serves **4**
nutritional count per serving **31.2g total fat**
(16.4g saturated fat); 2312kJ (553 cal);
31.1g carbohydrate; 33.9g protein; 7.1g fibre

250g cherry tomatoes
cooking-oil spray
6 rashers rindless bacon (390g)
1 small french bread stick (150g)
180g bocconcini cheese, halved
1 large cos lettuce, leaves torn
mustard mayonnaise
⅓ cup (100g) mayonnaise
2 teaspoons wholegrain mustard
¼ cup (60ml) lemon juice

1 Make mustard mayonnaise.
2 Preheat grill.
3 Place tomatoes on oven tray; spray with oil.
Grill until softened slightly. Cover to keep warm.
4 Grill bacon until crisp. Chop coarsely.
5 Cut bread into 8 slices; toast under grill until
browned both sides.
6 Combine tomato, bacon, cheese and lettuce
in large bowl. Divide among serving dishes;
drizzle with mayonnaise. Serve salad with toast.
mustard mayonnaise Combine ingredients in
small bowl.

blt salad

ROCKET, PROSCIUTTO AND EGG SALAD

prep & cook time **25 minutes** serves **4**

Pan-fry 8 slices prosciutto until crisp; chop coarsely. Cut four hard-boiled eggs in half. Divide 120g baby rocket leaves and eggs among plates. Sprinkle with prosciutto and ¼ cup shaved parmesan cheese. Serve drizzled with ½ cup caesar dressing.

BEEF, BEETROOT AND WITLOF SALAD

prep & cook time **30 minutes** serves **4**

Cook 600g piece eye fillet on heated oiled grill plate (or grill or barbecue) until cooked as desired. Cover; stand 10 minutes then cut into 1cm-thick slices. Place beef in large bowl with leaves of 2 trimmed white witlof, ¾ cup roasted pecans and 450g can drained baby beetroot; toss gently then sprinkle over 120g crumbled soft goats cheese. Whisk ¼ cup olive oil and 1 tablespoon wholegrain mustard in small jug; drizzle dressing over salad.

FAST MEAT SALADS

TURKEY FIG AND SPINACH SALAD

prep time **10 minutes** serves **4**

Combine 2 tablespoons raspberry vinegar and
2 teaspoons walnut oil in screw-top jar; shake
well. Quarter 6 large fresh figs; combine in
large bowl with 100g baby spinach leaves,
100g coarsely chopped shaved turkey breast
and dressing, toss gently.

CHAR SIU PORK SALAD

prep & cook time **30 minutes** serves **4**

Grate 1 teaspoon rind from 1 of 2 large oranges;
segment both oranges over large bowl. Reserve
⅓ cup juice; discard the remainder. Combine
2 tablespoons reserved juice with rind, ¼ cup
char siu sauce, 1 finely chopped fresh red thai
chilli and 600g pork fillet in medium bowl. Cook
pork, uncovered, in heated oiled large frying
pan. Cover; stand 5 minutes then slice thickly.
Place pork in bowl with orange segments; mix
in remaining juice, 2 tablespoons olive oil and
200g mizuna. Serve topped with ¼ cup
chopped roasted unsalted peanuts.

pork and caramelised apple salad

PORK AND CARAMELISED APPLE SALAD

prep & cook time **30 minutes** serves **4**
nutritional count per serving **23.8g total fat**
(5.1g saturated fat); 1639kJ (392 cal);
10.6g carbohydrate; 33.5g protein; 1.1g fibre

600g pork fillet
2 tablespoons brown sugar
2 teaspoons wholegrain mustard
2 teaspoons finely grated orange rind
1 tablespoon olive oil
10g butter
1 medium green-skinned apple (150g),
    unpeeled, halved, cut into 5mm-thick slices
60g baby spinach leaves
spiced orange dressing
¼ cup (60ml) olive oil
2 tablespoons orange juice
1 tablespoon cider vinegar
1 teaspoon mixed spice

1 Combine pork, sugar, mustard and rind in
medium bowl.
2 Heat oil in medium frying pan; cook pork
until cooked as desired. Cover pork; stand
5 minutes then slice thinly.
3 Melt butter in same frying pan; cook apple
until caramelised.
4 Meanwhile, make spiced orange dressing.
5 Combine apple mixture, dressing and
spinach in medium bowl. Arrange pork among
serving plates; top with apple salad. Drizzle
with any remaining dressing from bowl.
spiced orange dressing Combine ingredients
in screw-top jar; shake well.

FIVE-SPICE PORK AND NASHI IN CHILLI PLUM DRESSING

prep & cook time **30 minutes**
(+ refrigeration) serves **4**
nutritional count per serving **14.8g total fat**
(4.3g saturated fat); 1522kJ (364 cal);
22.5g carbohydrate; 33.3g protein; 3.1g fibre

600g pork fillets
2 teaspoons vegetable oil
1 teaspoon five-spice powder

five-spice pork and nashi in
chilli plum dressing

300g mizuna
2 green onions, sliced thinly
2 medium nashi (400g), sliced thinly
chilli plum dressing
¼ cup (60ml) plum sauce
1 tablespoon water
1 tablespoon lemon juice
1 fresh long red chilli, sliced thinly

1 Combine pork, oil and five-spice in large
bowl; refrigerate 3 hours or overnight.
2 Make chilli plum dressing.
3 Cook pork on heated oiled grill plate (or grill
or barbecue) until cooked as desired. Cover;
stand 10 minutes then slice thickly.
4 Combine mizuna, onion and nashi in large
bowl with two-thirds of the dressing. Serve
salad topped with pork; drizzle with remaining
chilli plum dressing.
chilli plum dressing Combine ingredients in
screw-top jar; shake well.

chorizo, roasted capsicum and
artichoke salad

CHORIZO, ROASTED CAPSICUM AND ARTICHOKE SALAD

prep & cook time **25 minutes** serves **4**
nutritional count per serving **36g total fat**
(10.8g saturated fat); 1885kJ (451 cal);
16.4g carbohydrate; 20.5g protein; 3.9g fibre

2 large red capsicums (700g)
2 chorizo sausages (340g), sliced thinly
280g jar artichoke hearts in brine,
    drained, halved
200g red grape tomatoes, halved
80g curly endive leaves
½ cup firmly packed fresh flat-leaf
    parsley leaves
herb and garlic dressing
2 tablespoons olive oil
2 tablespoons white wine vinegar
1 tablespoon lemon juice
1 tablespoon finely chopped fresh basil
1 tablespoon finely chopped fresh oregano
2 cloves garlic, chopped finely

1 Quarter capsicums; discard seeds and
membranes. Roast capsicum under hot grill,
skin-side up, until skin blisters and blackens.
Cover capsicum pieces with plastic or paper
for 5 minutes; peel away skin then cut pieces
in half diagonally.
2 Meanwhile, cook chorizo in large frying pan,
stirring occasionally, until browned. Drain on
absorbent paper.
3 Make herb and garlic dressing.
4 Combine capsicum, chorizo, dressing and
remaining ingredients in large bowl.
herb and garlic dressing Combine
ingredients in small bowl.

BROWN LENTIL, ZUCCHINI AND CHORIZO SALAD

prep & cook time **30 minutes** serves **4**
nutritional count per serving **39.8g total fat**
(11.2g saturated fat); 2161kJ (517 cal);
13.9g carbohydrate; 24.1g protein; 6.2g fibre

2 chorizo sausages (340g), sliced thinly
1 large zucchini (150g), sliced thinly
    lengthways
2 x 400g cans brown lentils, rinsed, drained
250g red grape tomatoes, halved
1 cup loosely packed fresh flat-leaf
    parsley leaves
cajun dressing
¼ cup (60ml) olive oil
1 tablespoon red wine vinegar
2 tablespoons cajun spice mix

1 Cook chorizo and zucchini on heated oiled
grill plate (or grill or barbecue) until chorizo is
cooked and zucchini is tender.
2 Meanwhile, make cajun dressing.
3 Combine chorizo, zucchini, dressing and
remaining ingredients in large bowl.
cajun dressing Combine ingredients in
screw-top jar; shake well.

WATERMELON, MINT & FETTA SALAD

prep time 10 minutes **serves** 4
nutritional count per serving 6.2g total fat
(3.8g saturated fat); 506kJ (121 cal);
10.1g carbohydrate; 5.4g protein; 1.5g fibre

2 teaspoons white sugar
¼ cup (60ml) lime juice
½ cup (100g) crumbled fetta cheese
½ small red onion (50g), sliced thinly
½ cup coarsely chopped fresh mint
850g seedless watermelon, cut into wedges

1 Dissolve sugar in small jug with juice.
2 Combine juice in large bowl with cheese,
onion and mint; spoon over watermelon.

notes Don't chop the mint until just before making
the salad as it blackens and goes limp once cut.
We used a fairly bland fetta cheese here so its
flavour didn't overpower the melon.

CHEESE, EGG & VEGIE SALADS

warm kipfler potato salad

MOROCCAN ORANGE & RADISH SALAD

prep time **20 minutes (+ refrigeration)** serves **4**
nutritional count per serving **0.3g total fat**
(0g saturated fat); 447kJ (107 cal);
20.1g carbohydrate; 3g protein; 5.2g fibre

10 trimmed medium red radishes (150g),
    sliced thinly
4 large oranges (1.2kg), segmented
1 small red onion (100g), sliced thinly
2 tablespoons coarsely chopped fresh
    flat-leaf parsley
2 tablespoons coarsely chopped
    fresh coriander
¼ cup (60ml) orange juice

1 Assemble radish, orange and onion on
serving platter; sprinkle with parsley and
coriander, drizzle with juice.
2 Cover salad; refrigerate 1 hour before serving.

WARM KIPFLER POTATO SALAD

prep & cook time **30 minutes** serves **4**
nutritional count per serving **14g total fat**
(1.9g saturated fat); 1267kJ (303 cal);
34.4g carbohydrate; 6.8g protein; 6.2g fibre

1kg kipfler potatoes, unpeeled,
    halved lengthways
¼ cup (60ml) olive oil
1 teaspoon finely grated lemon rind
1 tablespoon lemon juice
2 teaspoons wholegrain mustard
1 small red onion (100g), sliced thinly
1 cup loosely packed fresh flat-leaf parsley

1 Boil, steam or microwave potato until
tender; drain.
2 Whisk oil, rind, juice and mustard in large
bowl; mix in potatoes, onion and parsley.

moroccan orange & radish salad

tabbouleh

TABBOULEH

prep time **30 minutes (+ refrigeration)** serves **4**
nutritional count per serving **14.1g total fat**
(2g saturated fat); 790kJ (189 cal);
9.2g carbohydrate; 3.4g protein; 5.6g fibre

¼ cup (40g) burghul
3 medium tomatoes (450g)
3 cups coarsely chopped fresh
   flat-leaf parsley
3 green onions, chopped finely
¼ cup coarsely chopped fresh mint
¼ cup (60ml) lemon juice
¼ cup (60ml) olive oil

1 Place burghul in medium shallow bowl.
Halve tomatoes, scoop pulp from tomato over
burghul. Chop tomato flesh finely; spread over
burghul. Cover; refrigerate 1 hour.
2 Combine burghul mixture in large bowl with
remaining ingredients.

green bean & tomato salad

GREEN BEAN & TOMATO SALAD

prep & cook time **20 minutes** serves **4**
nutritional count per serving **20.2g total fat**
(1.8g saturated fat); 920kJ (220 cal);
3.6g carbohydrate; 4.2g protein; 4.3g fibre

200g green beans, trimmed
250g cherry tomatoes, halved
mustard hazelnut dressing
½ cup (70g) roasted hazelnuts, skinned,
   chopped coarsely
2 tablespoons hazelnut oil
2 tablespoons cider vinegar
1 teaspoon wholegrain mustard

1 Make mustard hazelnut dressing.
2 Boil, steam or microwave beans until tender;
drain. Rinse under cold water; drain.
3 Combine beans, tomato and dressing in
medium bowl; toss gently.
mustard hazelnut dressing Combine
ingredients in screw-top jar; shake well.

CAPRESE SALAD

prep time **15 minutes** serves **4**

Thinly slice 3 large egg tomatoes and 300g
drained bocconcini cheese; overlap slices
on serving platter. Drizzle with 2 tablespoons
olive oil; sprinkle with ¼ cup firmly packed
then torn fresh basil leaves.

GREEK SALAD

prep time **15 minutes** serves **4**

Combine 4 thinly sliced medium egg tomatoes,
2 thinly sliced lebanese cucumbers, ½ cup
seeded kalamata olives, 1 thinly sliced small red
onion and 150g coarsely chopped fetta cheese
in large bowl. Combine 2 tablespoons olive oil,
2 tablespoons lemon juice and 2 teaspoons
fresh oregano leaves in screw-top jar; shake
well. Drizzle dressing over salad.

FAST VEGIE SALADS

PEAR, WALNUT & FETTA SALAD

prep time **20 minutes** serves **4**

Combine 1 tablespoon walnut oil, 2 teaspoons wholegrain mustard, 2 tablespoons white wine vinegar and 1 tablespoon finely chopped fresh chives in screw-top jar; shake well. Separate leaves of 1 butter lettuce then tear roughly. Core 1 unpeeled medium pear then slice into thin wedges. Combine lettuce, pear and dressing in large bowl with ⅓ cup coarsely chopped roasted walnuts, 40g trimmed snow pea sprouts, 50g crumbled fetta cheese and 35g shaved parmesan cheese; toss gently.

COS, AVOCADO & TOMATO SALAD

prep time **15 minutes** serves **4**

Separate the leaves of 1 baby cos lettuce. Reserve several of the larger leaves; shred remaining leaves coarsely. Combine 3 finely chopped medium tomatoes, 2 finely chopped medium avocados, 1 finely chopped lebanese cucumber, 1 finely chopped small red onion, ¼ cup coarsely chopped fresh coriander, ¼ cup lime juice and 2 crushed garlic cloves in medium bowl; add shredded lettuce, toss gently. Serve salad divided among reserved leaves.

pan-fried haloumi with green salad

PAN-FRIED HALOUMI WITH GREEN SALAD

prep & cook time **20 minutes** serves **4**
nutritional count per serving **12g** total fat
(7g saturated fat); 949kJ (227 cal);
11.8g carbohydrate; 17.3g protein; 5.4g fibre

150g curly endive
50g baby spinach leaves
½ cup loosely packed fresh flat-leaf
    parsley leaves
⅔ cup (125g) drained semi-dried tomatoes,
    chopped coarsely
250g haloumi cheese
lemon dijon dressing
¼ cup (60ml) lemon juice
1 clove garlic, crushed
1 tablespoon water
1 teaspoon white sugar
1 teaspoon dijon mustard
¼ teaspoon ground cumin
pinch cayenne pepper

1 Combine endive, spinach, parsley and
tomato in medium bowl.
2 Cut cheese into eight slices.
3 Heat lightly oiled medium frying pan; cook
cheese, in batches, until browned both sides.
4 Meanwhile, make lemon dijon dressing.
5 Add dressing to salad; toss gently. Serve
salad topped with cheese.
lemon dijon dressing Combine ingredients in
screw-top jar; shake well.

note **Haloumi must be cooked just before serving as it
becomes leathery and unpalatable when cold.**

waldorf salad

WALDORF SALAD

prep time **20 minutes** serves **4**
nutritional count per serving **35.7g** total fat
(3.1g saturated fat); 1852kJ (443 cal);
22.4g carbohydrate; 5.8g protein; 6.3g fibre

¾ cup (225g) mayonnaise
¼ cup (60ml) lemon juice
5 stalks celery (750g), trimmed, sliced thickly
2 medium red apples (300g), sliced thinly
1 small red onion (100g), sliced thinly
1 cup (100g) roasted walnuts
1 cup loosely packed fresh flat-leaf
    parsley leaves

1 Combine mayonnaise and juice in large
bowl; mix in remaining ingredients.

CLASSIC FRENCH DRESSING

prep time **10 minutes** makes **1 cup**

Combine ¼ cup white vinegar, ¾ cup olive oil, ½ teaspoon white sugar and 1 teaspoon dijon mustard in screw-top jar; shake well.

THOUSAND ISLAND DRESSING

prep time **10 minutes** makes **1 cup**

Combine ½ cup mayonnaise, 1½ tablespoons tomato sauce, ½ small finely grated white onion, 8 finely chopped pimiento-stuffed green olives and ½ small finely chopped red capsicum in small bowl.

DRESSINGS

CLASSIC ITALIAN DRESSING

prep time **10 minutes** makes **1 cup**

Combine 2 tablespoons white wine vinegar,
2 tablespoons lemon juice, ½ teaspoon white
sugar, 2 crushed garlic cloves, ¾ cup olive oil,
1 tablespoon finely chopped fresh basil leaves
and 1 tablespoon finely chopped fresh oregano
leaves in screw-top jar; shake well.

MAYONNAISE

prep time **15 minutes** makes **1 cup**

Combine 2 egg yolks, ½ teaspoon salt and
1 teaspoon dijon mustard in medium bowl. Add
⅔ cup extra light olive oil and ⅓ cup olive oil in
a thin, steady stream, whisking constantly until
mixture thickens. Stir in 1 tablespoon white wine
vinegar and 1 tablespoon lemon juice.

ALMONDS, SLIVERED small thin lengthways-cut pieces.

ARTICHOKE HEARTS tender centre of the globe artichoke; purchased, in brine, canned or in glass jars.

BEANS

borlotti also known as roman or pink beans. Interchangeable with pinto beans because of their appearance – both are pale pink or beige with dark red streaks.

butter also known as lima beans; large, flat, kidney-shaped bean, off-white in colour, with a mealy texture and mild taste.

cannellini white bean similar in appearance and flavour to great northern, navy and haricot beans.

dried black also known as turtle beans or black kidney beans; an earthy-flavoured dried bean completely different from the better-known chinese black beans (which are fermented soya beans).

kidney medium-sized red bean, slightly floury in texture yet sweet in flavour.

mixed a canned mix of kidney beans, butter beans, chickpeas and cannellini beans.

BEETROOT (red beets or beets) a firm, round root vegetable.

BREADS

ciabatta a popular Italian white bread with a crisp crust.

french bread a long, thin, narrow roundish loaf. It usually has a crisp brown crust and light chewy interior. Also known as french loaf or baguette.

lavash (lavosh) flat, unleavened bread of Mediterranean origin.

pitta also known as lebanese bread. A pocket bread sold in large, flat pieces that separate into two thin rounds. Pocket pitta is also available.

BURGHUL also known as bulghur or bulgar wheat; hulled steamed wheat kernels. Not the same as cracked wheat.

BUTTERMILK originally the term given to the slightly sour liquid left after butter was churned from cream, today it is made similarly to yogurt. Sold alongside fresh milk products; despite its name, it is actually low in fat.

CAPERBERRIES fruit formed after the caper buds have flowered; usually pickled, with stalks intact.

CAPERS the grey-green buds of a Mediterranean-climate shrub, sold dried and salted or pickled in brine. Baby capers are fuller-flavoured than the full-sized ones. Capers must be rinsed well before using.

CAPSICUM also known as bell pepper or, simply, pepper.

CHEESE

blue these are mould-treated cheeses with blue veining. Varieties include firm and crumbly stilton types to mild, creamy brie-like cheeses.

bocconcini from the diminutive of 'boccone' meaning mouthful, a walnut-sized, baby mozzarella. A delicate, semi-soft, white cheese. Spoils rapidly so must be kept under refrigeration, in brine, for 1 or 2 days at most.

haloumi a firm, cream-coloured sheep-milk cheese matured in brine; somewhat like a minty, salty fetta in flavour. Should be eaten warm, as it becomes tough and rubbery on cooling.

CHERVIL also known as cicily; a herb with a mild fennel flavour.

CHILLI available in many different types and sizes. Use rubber gloves when seeding and chopping fresh chillies as they can burn your skin. Remove the seeds and membranes to lessen the heat level.

green any unripened chilli.

long red available both fresh and dried; a generic term used for any moderately hot, long (6cm-8cm), thin chilli.

red thai small, medium hot and bright red in colour.

CHORIZO a sausage of Spanish origin, made of coarsely ground pork and highly seasoned with garlic and chillies.

CORIANDER also known as pak chee, cilantro or chinese parsley; bright-green leafy herb with a pungent flavour. Both the stems and roots of coriander are used in Thai cooking; wash well before using. Also available ground or as seeds; these should not be substituted for fresh coriander as the tastes are completely different.

COUSCOUS a fine, grain-like cereal product made from dehydrated semolina.

CRANBERRIES, DRIED these have the same slightly sour, succulent flavour as fresh cranberries. Available in most major supermarkets.

GLOSSARY

CUCUMBER, LEBANESE short, slender and thin-skinned. Has tender, edible skin, tiny, yielding seeds, and a sweet, fresh taste.

CUMIN also known as zeera or comino.

FIVE-SPICE POWDER also known as chinese five-spice; a fragrant mixture of ground cinnamon, cloves, star anise, pepper and fennel seeds.

HARISSA a Moroccan sauce or paste made from dried chillies, cumin, garlic, oil and caraway seeds. Available from Middle-Eastern food shops and most major supermarkets.

HORSERADISH CREAM a prepared paste of horseradish, mustard seed, oil and sugar.

LYCHEES small fruit from China with a hard shell and sweet, juicy flesh. The white flesh has a gelatinous texture and musky, perfumed taste. Available both fresh and canned in syrup from supermarkets.

MUSTARD, DIJON pale brown, distinctively flavoured, fairly mild tasting french mustard.

MUSTARD SEEDS come in black, brown or yellow (white) varieties; black are more spicy and piquant than the others. Available from health-food shops and spice shops.

NASHI a member of the pear family but resembling an apple with its pale yellow-green, tennis-ball-sized appearance; more commonly known as the asian pear. It has a distinctive texture and mildly sweet taste.

NOODLES BEAN THREAD made from extruded mung bean paste; also known as cellophane or glass noodles because they're transparent when cooked.

OIL

hazelnut pressed from ground hazelnuts. Available from speciality food stores and some larger supermarkets.

olive made from ripened olives. Extra virgin and virgin are the best, while extra light or light refers to taste not fat levels.

peanut pressed from ground peanuts; most commonly used oil in Asian cooking because of its high smoke point (handles high heat without burning).

sesame made from roasted, crushed, white sesame seeds; mainly used as a flavouring rather than a cooking medium.

vegetable sourced from plants rather than animal fats.

walnut pressed from ground walnuts. Available from speciality food stores, delicatessens and some larger supermarkets.

OLIVES, PIMIENTO-STUFFED GREEN a green olive with a piquant, briny bitterness and stuffed with a morsel of capsicum, which adds a flash of colour. Available from delicatessens and most major supermarkets.

ONIONS

green also known as scallion or, incorrectly, shallot; an immature onion picked before the bulb has formed, having a long, bright-green edible stalk.

red also known as spanish, red spanish or bermuda onion. A large, sweet, purplish-red onion.

PAPRIKA ground dried sweet red capsicum (bell pepper); there are many types and grades available, including sweet, hot, mild and smoked.

PARSLEY, FLAT-LEAF also known as continental parsley or italian parsley.

PEPITAS edible pumpkin seeds with the white hull removed. Has a delicate nutty flavour.

PINE NUTS also known as pignoli; not in fact a nut but a small, cream-coloured kernel from pine cones.

PRAWNS also known as shrimp.

PROSCIUTTO cured, air-dried (unsmoked), pressed ham.

RED RADISH a peppery root vegetable related to the mustard plant. The small round red variety is the mildest, it is crisp and juicy, and usually eaten raw in salads.

RICE

basmati a white, fragrant long-grained rice. It should be washed several times before cooking.

wild rice blend a mixture of white long-grain and dark brown wild rice. The latter is the seed of a North American aquatic grass, which has a distinctively nutty flavour and a crunchy, resilient texture.

SALAD LEAVES

butter lettuce have small, round, loosely formed heads with soft, buttery-textured leaves. The flavour is sweet and succulent.

cos lettuce (romaine lettuce) the traditional caesar salad lettuce. Baby cos have tiny leaves. Available from most supermarkets and greengrocers.

curly endive also known as frisée (frisee); a curly-leafed green vegetable.

iceberg lettuce heavy with tightly packed crisp leaves.

lambs lettuce also known as mâche, corn salad or lamb tongue; tender narrow dark-green leaves having a mild, almost nutty flavour.

mesclun a salad mix of assorted young lettuce and other green leaves, including baby spinach leaves, mizuna and curly endive.

mizuna a feathery green salad leaf having a sharp, slightly mustardy flavour: found in most greengrocers.

oak leaf also known as feville de chenel; available in both red and green leaf varieties.

rocket also known as arugula, rugula and rucola; a peppery-tasting green leaf that can be used similarly to baby spinach leaves, eaten raw in salad or used in cooking. Baby rocket (wild rocket) leaves are both smaller and less peppery.

spinach also known as english spinach and, incorrectly, silver beet. Its dark green leaves can be eaten raw or cooked.

watercress also known as winter rocket. Is one of the cress family, a large group of peppery greens.

witlof also known as chicory or belgian endive.

SALMON, SMOKED is one of the most popular types of smoked fish; it is made by placing the fish in brine, curing it in salt and sugar and then smoking it over wood chips.

SAMBAL OELEK (also spelled ulek or olek) a salty paste made from chillies and vinegar.

SAUCES

char siu a Chinese barbecue sauce made from sugar, water, salt, fermented soya bean paste, honey, soy sauce, malt syrup and spices.

fish also called nam pla or nuoc nam; made from pulverised salted fermented fish, usually anchovies. Has a pungent smell and strong taste, so use according to your taste.

soy also known as sieu, is made from fermented soya beans. We use a mild Japanese variety in our recipes, unless otherwise stated.

light soy a fairly thin, pale but salty tasting sauce. Not the same as salt-reduced or low-sodium soy.

sweet chilli a mild, Thai-type sauce made from red chillies, sugar, garlic and vinegar.

SNOW PEAS also called mange tout ("eat all").

SUGAR

caster also known as superfine or finely granulated table sugar.

palm also known as nam tan pip, jaggery, jawa or gula melaka; made from the sap of the sugar palm tree. Usually sold in rock-hard cakes. Use brown sugar, if palm sugar is unavailable.

white a coarsely granulated table sugar, also known as crystal sugar.

SULTANAS dried grapes, also known as golden raisins.

SUMAC a purple-red, astringent spice ground from berries growing on shrubs that flourish wild around the Mediterranean; adds a tart, lemony flavour.

TAMARIND CONCENTRATE the distillation of tamarind pulp into a condensed paste. Used straight from the container, with no soaking or straining required.

VIETNAMESE MINT not a mint at all, but a pungent, peppery narrow-leafed member of the buckwheat family; also known as cambodian mint and laksa leaf.

VINEGAR

balsamic made from the juice of Trebbiano grapes; it is a deep rich brown colour with a sweet and sour flavour.

white balsamic vinegar (condiment) is a colourless version of balsamic vinegar; has a fresh, sweet taste.

cider (apple cider) made from fermented apples.

raspberry raspberries steeped in a white wine vinegar.

red wine based on fermented red wine.

white made from cane sugar.

white wine made from a blend of white wines.

WOMBOK also known as peking cabbage, chinese cabbage or petsai. Elongated in shape with pale green, crinkly leaves; popular in South-East Asia.

ZUCCHINI also known as courgette.

CONVERSION CHART

MEASURES

One Australian metric measuring cup holds approximately 250ml, one Australian metric tablespoon holds 20ml, one Australian metric teaspoon holds 5ml.

The difference between one country's measuring cups and another's is within a 2- or 3-teaspoon variance, and will not affect your cooking results. North America, New Zealand and the United Kingdom use a 15ml tablespoon. All cup and spoon measurements are level. The most accurate way of measuring dry ingredients is to weigh them. When measuring liquids, use a clear glass or plastic jug with metric markings.

We use large eggs with an average weight of 60g.

DRY MEASURES

METRIC	IMPERIAL
15g	½oz
30g	1oz
60g	2oz
90g	3oz
125g	4oz (¼lb)
155g	5oz
185g	6oz
220g	7oz
250g	8oz (½lb)
280g	9oz
315g	10oz
345g	11oz
375g	12oz (¾lb)
410g	13oz
440g	14oz
470g	15oz
500g	16oz (1lb)
750g	24oz (1½lb)
1kg	32oz (2lb)

LIQUID MEASURES

METRIC	IMPERIAL
30ml	1 fluid oz
60ml	2 fluid oz
100ml	3 fluid oz
125ml	4 fluid oz
150ml	5 fluid oz (¼ pint/1 gill)
190ml	6 fluid oz
250ml	8 fluid oz
300ml	10 fluid oz (½ pint)
500ml	16 fluid oz
600ml	20 fluid oz (1 pint)
1000ml (1 litre)	1¾ pints

LENGTH MEASURES

METRIC	IMPERIAL
3mm	⅛in
6mm	¼in
1cm	½in
2cm	¾in
2.5cm	1in
5cm	2in
6cm	2½in
8cm	3in
10cm	4in
13cm	5in
15cm	6in
18cm	7in
20cm	8in
23cm	9in
25cm	10in
28cm	11in
30cm	12in (1ft)

OVEN TEMPERATURES

These oven temperatures are only a guide for conventional ovens.
For fan-forced ovens, check the manufacturer's manual.

	°C (CELSIUS)	°F (FAHRENHEIT)	GAS MARK
Very slow	120	250	½
Slow	150	275-300	1-2
Moderately slow	160	325	3
Moderate	180	350-375	4-5
Moderately hot	200	400	6
Hot	220	425-450	7-8
Very hot	240	475	9

INDEX

ACP BOOKS

General manager Christine Whiston
Editor-in-chief Susan Tomnay
Creative director Hieu Chi Nguyen
Art director Hannah Blackmore
Designer Clare O'Loughlin
Senior editor Wendy Bryant
Food director Pamela Clark
Sales & rights director Brian Cearnes
Marketing manager Bridget Cody
Senior business analyst Rebecca Varela
Circulation manager Jama Mclean
Operations manager David Scotto
Production manager Victoria Jefferys

ACP Books are published by ACP Magazines
a division of PBL Media Pty Limited
PBL Media, Chief Executive officer Ian Law
Publishing & sales director, Women's lifestyle Lynette Phillips
Editor-at-large, Women's lifestyle Pat Ingram
Marketing director, Women's lifestyle Matthew Dominello
Commercial manager, Women's lifestyle Seymour Cohen
Research Director, Women's lifestyle Justin Stone

Produced by ACP Books, Sydney.

Published by ACP Books, a division of ACP Magazines Ltd, 54 Park St, Sydney; GPO Box 4088, Sydney, NSW 2001.
phone (02) 9282 8618; fax (02) 9267 9438. acpbooks@acpmagazines.com.au; www.acpbooks.com.au

Printed by Toppan Printing Co., China.

Australia Distributed by Network Services, phone +61 2 9282 8777;
fax +61 2 9264 3278; networkweb@networkservicescompany.com.au
United Kingdom Distributed by Australian Consolidated Press (UK),
phone (01604) 642 200; fax (01604) 642 300; books@acpuk.com
New Zealand Distributed by Netlink Distribution Company,
phone (9) 366 9966; ask@ndc.co.nz
South Africa Distributed by PSD Promotions, phone (27 11) 392 6065/6/7;
fax (27 11) 392 6079/80; orders@psdprom.co.za
Canada Distributed by Publishers Group Canada
phone (800) 663 5714; fax (800) 565 3770; service@raincoast.com

Title: Simple salads / food director Pamela Clark.
ISBN: 978 1 86396 858 4 (pbk.)
Notes: Includes index.
Subjects: Salads. Cookery.
Other Authors/Contributors: Clark, Pamela.
Dewey Number: 641.83
© ACP Magazines Ltd 2009
ABN 18 053 273 546

Cover Salad niçoise, page 24
Photographer Luke Burgess
Stylist Kate Murdoch
Food preparation Kellie-Marie Thomas

Send recipe enquiries to: recipeenquiries@acpmagazines.com.au